The Ultimate

Musicals

Crossword Collection

KYLE BECKER

INTRODUCTION

Welcome to the Ultimate Musicals Crossword Collection. This book contains over 35 crosswords all themed around Musicals.

Happy Puzzling!

Act 1

CROSSWORD 1

Across

1 *Meet Me in St Louis* song; 'The _____ Song' (7)

4 *James and the Giant Peach* song; 'On Your Way ____' (4)

7 Lead character in *Kiss Me, Kate* (5)

9 Lead character in *Seussical* (4)

10 Donna and Sophie's surname in *Mamma Mia!* (8)

12 *La Cage Aux Folles* song; 'With ____ on My Arm' (4)

13 Lead character in *Fame* (5)

14 Lead character in *A Funny Thing Happened on the Way to the Forum* (6)

15 *A Year with Frog and Toad* song; 'Toad to the _____' (6)

16 Character played by Chloe Dallimore in musical movie *Annie* (2011) (4)

17 Actor playing Ali Boloorchi in musical movie *The Music Man* (2007) (6,5)

19 Wrote the lyrics to *Spamalot* (4,4)

20 *Hairspray* song; 'Big, _____ & Beautiful' (6)

22 Lead character in *Big*; _____ Lawrence (5)

23 Sky and Nathan are the 'Guys'; Sarah and Miss Adelaide are the '____' (5)

24 *Grease* song; 'Greased _____' (9)

Down

1 Character played by John Leguizamo in musical movie *Moulin Rouge!* (2001) (8,7)

2 Annie's surname in *Annie Get Your Gun* (6)

3 Actor voicing Audrey II in musical movie *Little Shop of Horrors* (1986) (4,6)

4 Lead character in *Annie* played by Nancye Hayes in 2011 musical movie; Miss _____ (8)

5 Character played by Mikaela Kennerly in musical movie *Oklahoma!* (2013) (5)

6 Surname of Danny in the musical *Grease* (4)

8 Actress playing Luisa in musical movie *The Fantasticks* (2000); _____ _____ Kelly (4,6)

9 Character played by John Kerr in musical movie *South Pacific* (1958) (6,5)

11 Actress playing Claire Huddesen in musical movie *On the Town* (1949) (3,6)

13 Character played by Danny Glover in musical movie *Dreamgirls* (2006) (5,7)

18 Lead character in *Cry-Baby the Musical* (7)

20 *Brigadoon* song; 'Come to Me, ____ to Me' (4)

21 Lead character in *Ain't Misbehavin'* (4)

CROSSWORD 2

CROSSWORD 3

Across

1 *The Lion King* song; '_____ of Life' (6)

6 *Billy Elliot* song; '_____'s Song' (7)

8 Lead character in *Mean Girls* (6)

10 Lead character in *BEEHIVE: The 1960's Musical* (5)

11 Lead character in *Chicago* (5,4)

13 *She Loves Me* song; 'A Trip to the _____' (7)

15 Lead character in *Les Misérables* (7)

16 Actor voicing Kristoff in musical movie *Frozen* (2013) (8,5)

18 *Heathers the Musical* song; '_____ Store' (5)

19 Character played by Hugh Jackman in musical movie *The Greatest Showman* (2017) (1,1,6)

20 *Camelot* song; 'If Ever I Would _____ You' (5)

21 Lead character in *Bat Out of Hell: The Musical* (5)

22 Lead character in *Aspects of Love* (4)

24 Lead character in *Bullets over Broadway*; ____ Sinclair (5)

25 *Cinderella* song; 'The Loneliness of _____' (7)

26 James Early's nickname in *Dreamgirls* (7)

Down

1 Show that takes its name from a fairground attraction (8)

2 Lead character in *Rent* (5)

3 *The Wedding Singer* song; 'A Note From _____' (5)

4 Japanese city where *Madame Butterfly* is set (8)

5 Director of movie musical *Funny Girl* (2018) (6,8)

7 Supporting character in *Cats*; Old _____ (11)

9 Musical with characters from the Houseman family and Johnny Castle (5,7)

12 Actor playing Horace Vandergelder in musical movie *Hello, Dolly!* (1969) (6,7)

14 *Meet Me in St Louis* song; 'Over the _____' (9)

15 Director of movie musical *Beauty and the Beast* (1987) (6,6)

16 Lead character in *If/Then* (4)

17 *Name the musical movie*: An Irish immigrant and his daughter move into a town in the American South with a magical piece of gold (1968); _____'s Rainbow (6)

20 Character played by Oscar Levant in musical movie *The Band Wagon* (1953); ____ Marton (6)

21 *The 25th Annual Putnam County Spelling Bee* song; 'The I Love You _____' (4)

23 The daughter of George and Winifred in *Mary Poppins* (4)

CROSSWORD 4

Across

6 Lead character in *Hairspray* (7)

8 One of Henry VIII's wives in *Six* (4,6)

10 Lead character in *Pretty Woman: The Musical* (6)

11 Actress playing Betty Haynes in musical movie *White Christmas* (1954) (8,7)

13 One of the Moe's in *Five Guys Named Moe* (2,3)

14 *Evita* song; 'Don't Cry for Me, _____' (9)

15 Composer of movie *Aladdin* (2019); Alan _____ (6)

16 *Name the musical movie*: A silent film production company and cast make a difficult transition to sound (1952); *Singin' in the* _____ (4)

17 Family name in *Freaky Friday* (5)

19 Lead character in *Into the Woods* (3,5)

21 Lead character in *BEEHIVE: The 1960's Musical* (6)

22 *My Fair Lady* song; 'I Could Have _____ All Night' (6)

24 Character played by Jennifer Harding in musical movie *Funny Girl* (2018) (4)

25 Lead character in *A Day in Hollywood, A Night in the Ukraine* (4)

26 *42nd Street* song; 'About a Quarter to _____' (4)

27 *Jesus Christ Superstar* song; 'King _____'s Song' (5)

Down

1 Director of movie musical *Moulin Rouge!* (2001) (3,8)

2 Lead character in *Les Misérables* played by Hugh Jackman in 2012 musical movie version (4,7)

3 Song from *The Greatest Showman* musical movie; 'A _____ Dreams' (7)

4 Actress playing Julie LaVerne in musical movie *Show Boat* (1951) (3,7)

5 Actress playing Carole Hill in musical movie *Night and Day* (1946) (5,5)

7 Actor playing Avigdor in musical movie *Yentl* (1983) (5,8)

9 Another one of the Moe's in *Five Guys Named Moe* (3,3)

12 Director of movie musical *Porgy and Bess* (1959) (4,9)

15 *Chicago* song; 'When You're Good to _____' (4)

17 Actor playing Older Patrick in musical movie *Mame* (1974); _____ Davison (5)

18 *Name the musical movie*: A kind-hearted street urchin fights for a magic lamp that has the power to make your deepest wishes come true (1992) (7)

19 Number of Sophie's dads in *Mamma Mia* (5)

20 And another one of the Moe's in *Five Guys Named Moe* (3,3)

23 *Tommy* character; The _____ Queen (4)

CROSSWORD 5

Across

1 *Spring Awakening* song; 'Mama Who
   ____ Me' (4)
3 *Everybody's Talking About Jamie* song;
   'The ____ In My Head' (4)
8 *Grease* song; 'Born to Hand ____'
   (4)
9 Lead character in *West Side Story* (5)
10 Lead character in *Movin' Out* (5)
11 One of the sisters in *Frozen* (4)
14 Director of movie musical *Fiddler on
   the Roof* (1971) and *Jesus Christ
   Superstar* (1973) (6,7)
17 *Fame* song; 'Think of ____' (5,6)
18 Lead character in *BEEHIVE: The
   1960's Musical* (4)
19 *Avenue Q* song; 'There's a ____,
   Fine Line' (4)
21 Played the part of Danny Zuko in
   the London Premiere of *Grease* in
   1973; Richard ____ (4)
23 *Name the musical movie*: A nightclub
   performer hires a naive chorus girl
   to become his new dance partner
   (1948) (6,6)
24 Lead character in *West Side Story* (4)
25 *Grease* song; 'Look at Me, I'm
   ____' (6,3)
27 Lead character in *Merrily We Roll
   Along* (4,5)

Down

1 Lead character in *1776*; ____
   Franklin (8)
2 *The Fantasticks* song; 'Try to ____'
   (8)
4 *Aspects of* ____; Andrew Lloyd
   Webber musical (4)
5 Actress playing Gaby Duval in
   musical movie *Anything Goes* (1956)
   (4,9)
6 Lead character in *The Rocky Horror
   Show* (4,6)
7 Janet's surname in *The Rocky Horror
   Show* (5)
8 Character played by Elaine Stewart
   in musical movie *Brigadoon* (1954)
   (4,6)
12 *Fiddler on the Roof* song; 'Sunrise,
   ____' (6)
13 Lead character in *A Christmas Story:
   The Musical* (7)
15 Category of award received by Sir
   Elton John at the Academy Awards
   for *The Lion King*; Best ____
   ____ (8,4)
16 Actor playing Franz Liebkind in
   musical movie *The Producers* (2005)
   (4,7)
20 Surname of Frederick in *A Little
   Night Music* (7)
22 Baboon character in *The Lion King*
   (6)
26 Christine's surname in *The Phantom
   of the Opera* (4)

CROSSWORD 6

Across

1 *Evita* song; 'Another _____ in Another Hall' (8)

5 *The Pirates of Penzance* song; 'How Beautifully ____ the Sky' (4)

6 Director of musical movie *Rocketman* (2019) (6,8)

11 Actor playing Jimmy Smith in musical movie *Thoroughly Modern Millie* (1967) (5,3)

12 Lead character in *Hairspray* (5)

13 Character played by Ben Whishaw in musical movie *Mary Poppins Returns* (2018) (7,5)

15 Actress playing Hadass in musical movie *Yentl* (1983) (3,6)

16 *Little Shop of Horrors* song; '____ Me' (4)

17 Lead character in *A Funny Thing Happened on the Way to the Forum* played by Michael Crawford in 1966 movie (4)

18 *Bells are Ringing* song; 'The Party's ____' (4)

20 *The Bodyguard* song; 'All At ____' (4)

21 *Name the musical movie*: A Jewish peasant contends with marrying off three of his daughters (1971); *Fiddler on the* ____ (4)

22 Musical including songs 'Where Is Love?', 'Consider Yourself' and 'Oom-Pah-Pah' (6)

25 Lead character in *Movin' Out* (4)

27 *Meet Me in St Louis* song; 'Touch of the ____' (5)

28 Lead character in *La Cage Aux Folles* (5)

29 *Dreamgirls* song; 'One Night ____' (4)

30 *Whistle Down the Wind* song; 'A ____ is a Terrible Thing to Waste' (4)

Down

1 Lead character in *Fame* (6)

2 *The King and I* song; 'I Whistle a Happy ____' (4)

3 *Kinky Boots* song; '____ of a Man' (4)

4 Character played by Wilfrid Hyde-White in musical movie *My Fair Lady* (1964); Colonel ____ Pickering (4)

7 *Name the musical movie*: Dorothy Gale is swept away from a farm in Kansas to a magical land (1939) (3,6,2,2)

8 Character played by Cyd Charisse in musical movie *Brigadoon* (1954) (5)

9 Lead character in *Peter Pan* (7,4)

10 Lead character in *Anything Goes* (4,7)

11 Lead character in *Carousel* (5)

14 *The Secret Garden* song; 'A Bit of ____' (5)

16 Lead character in *Shrek the Musical*; Lord _____ (8)

19 Actress playing Parthenia Ann Hawks in musical movie *Show Boat* (1929); ____ Fitzroy (5)

23 Lead character in *Phantom* (4)

24 One of the three musketeers in *The Three Musketeers* (5)

26 Best friend and love interest of main character in *The Lion King* (4)

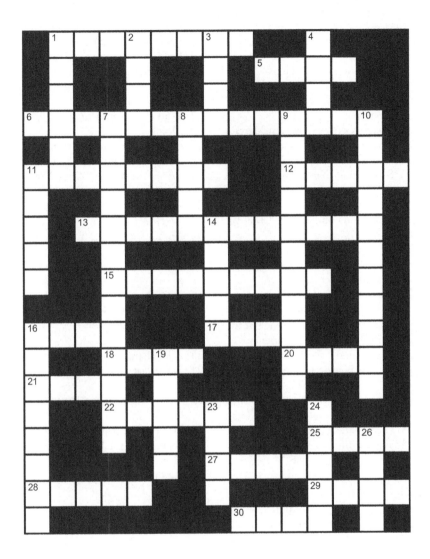

CROSSWORD 7

Across

1 *Willy Wonka* song; 'Think _____'
(8)

6 *Titanic* song; 'Mr Andrews' _____'
(6)

10 *Young Frankenstein* song; '_____
Love' (4)

11 Character played by Ann-Margret
in musical movie *Tommy* (1975) (4)

12 *West Side Story* song; Country (7)

13 Supporting character in *Avenue Q*
(5)

15 In *La Cage Aux Folles*, the type of
establishment that is La Cage Aux
Folles (9)

18 Actor playing Jafar in movie
Aladdin (2019) (6,7)

22 Lead character in *9 to 5* (6)

23 *Name the musical movie:* An
adaptation of *The Wizard of Oz* that
tries to capture the essence of the
African American experience
(1978) (3,3)

24 Actress playing Lynne in musical
movie *Godspell* (1973) (5,7)

26 Character played by Diego Boneta
in movie *Rock of Ages* (2012) (4,5)

28 Lead character in *Camelot* (9)

29 *The Best Little Whorehouse in Texas*
song; 'The _____' (8)

Down

2 Actor playing Pooh-Bah in musical
movie *The Mikado* (1939) (6,9)

3 *Cats* was based on the work of this
famous poet (2,5)

4 Lead character in *13* (4)

5 Character played by Zac Efron in
musical movie *The Greatest Showman*
(2017); Phillip _____ (7)

7 Lead character in *Chess*; _____
Molokov (4)

8 Bill Sykes' mistress in *Oliver!* played
by Shani Wallis in 1968 movie (5)

9 *The Producers* song; 'When You've
Got It, _____ It' (6)

14 Surname of Charlie in *Charlie and the
Chocolate Factory* (6)

16 *Kiss Me, Kate* song; 'Brush Up Your
_____' (11)

17 Actress playing Miss Adelaide in
musical movie *Guys and Dolls* (1955)
(6,6)

19 Actor playing Gaylord Ravenal in
musical movie *Show Boat* (1936)
(5,5)

20 Lead character in *Carousel* (6)

21 *Billy Elliot* song; 'Deep into the
_____' (6)

25 One of the gangs in *West Side Story*
(3,4)

27 Musical that features a song which
begins with the line 'Five hundred
twenty-five thousand six hundred
minutes' (4)

CROSSWORD 8

Across

2 Director of movie musical *The Pirates of Penzance* (1983) (7,5)

5 Name of the High School in *Grease* (6,4)

9 Lead character in *Aladdin* (5)

10 Lead character in *Jersey Boys* (4,5)

14 Lead character in *The Fantasticks* (4)

16 *Name the musical movie*: The story of the great female sharpshooter (1950) (5,3,4,3)

17 *Hamilton* character that practices French and plays piano with his mother (6)

18 Musical including songs 'All I Ask of You', 'Angel of Music' and 'Masquerade'; *The Phantom of the* ____ (5)

20 *Dirty Rotten Scoundrels* song; 'Great Big ____' (5)

21 Lead character in *Mamma Mia!* (5)

22 Character played by Emily Mortimer in musical movie *Mary Poppins Returns* (2018) (4,5)

24 Actor playing Laury in musical movie *A Chorus Line* (2016) (7,6)

25 Lead character in *Ghost the Musical*; Oda Mae ____ (5)

Down

1 Actor playing Sky Masterson in musical movie *Guys and Dolls* (1955) (6,6)

2 Lead character in *Cry-Baby the Musical* (4)

3 Lead character in *Kinky Boots* (4)

4 *Finding Neverland* song; 'Live by the ____' (4)

6 Main antagonist in *Frozen* (4)

7 *Name the musical movie*: A rich playboy and a youthful courtesan-in-training enjoy a platonic friendship in Paris (1958) (4)

8 *Name the musical movie*: A struggling female soprano finds work playing a male female impersonator, but it complicates her personal life (1982) (6,8)

11 Lead character in *The Book of Mormon* (5,5)

12 One of Henry VIII's wives in *Six*; Catherine of ____ (6)

13 Actor playing Andrew Carnes in musical movie *Oklahoma!* (2013) (5,5)

15 Actress playing Millie Dillmount in musical movie *Thoroughly Modern Millie* (1967) (5,7)

19 Character played by Nehemiah Persoff in musical movie *Yentl* (1983) (4)

20 Lady Gaga song from *A Star Is Born* that won the Oscar for Best Original Song in 2019 (7)

22 Name of the main horse in *War Horse* (4)

23 Lead character in *SpongeBob SquarePants* (5)

CROSSWORD 9

Across

3 *Hedwig and the Angry Inch* song; 'The Long _____' (5)

5 *Flashdance the Musical* song; 'My Next ____' (4)

7 Character played by Kelli O'Hara in musical movie *The King and I* (2018) (4)

8 Lead character in *High Society* (5,4)

9 Reindeer character in *Frozen* (4)

10 Character played by Julia Migenes in musical movie *Mack the Knife* (1989) (5,5)

13 *Six* song; 'Heart of _____' (5)

14 Character played by Sandro Dori in musical movie *Nine* (2009) (14)

16 Actor playing Bill Benson in musical movie *Anything Goes* (1956) (4,6)

19 Lead female character in *The Bodyguard* (6,6)

21 Lead character in *The Wiz* (4)

22 *Little Shop of Horrors* song; 'Somewhere That's _____' (5)

23 Character played by Richa Chadha in musical movie *Cabaret* (2019) (4)

24 *A Christmas Carol* song; 'Yesterday, _____ and Today' (8)

26 Actor playing Tony in musical movie *West Side Story* (1961) (7,6)

Down

1 *Oklahoma!* song; '_____ City' (6)

2 Character played by Eddie Barth in musical movie *Fame* (1980) (6)

4 Lead character in *Hairspray* (5)

6 *Jane Eyre* song; 'Painting Her _____' (8)

8 Lead character in *The Wiz* (3,3)

10 Composer of movie *Fiddler on the Roof* (1971) (5,4)

11 *How to Succeed in Business Without Really Trying* song; 'Happy to Keep His _____ Warm' (6)

12 Actress playing Guinevere in musical movie *Camelot* (1967) (7,8)

14 Surrogate parent for Buddy in *Elf* (5,5)

15 Actor playing Brankov in musical movie *Silk Stockings* (1957) (5,5)

17 Lead character in *Anne of Green Gables* (7)

18 *Name the musical movie*: A Jewish girl disguises herself as a boy to enter religious training (1983) (5)

20 Character played by Gladys Cooper in musical movie *The Happiest Millionaire* (1967) (4,4)

22 Kind of animal that Doctor Dillamond is in *Wicked* (4)

25 *The Rocky Horror Show* song; 'The Time ____' (4)

CROSSWORD 10

Across

1 Lead character in *A Tree Grows in Brooklyn* (5)

5 Lead character in *Aladdin* (5)

7 Lead character in *Jersey Boys* (5,6)

8 Character played by Michael Crawford in musical movie *Hello, Dolly!* (1969); Cornelius _____ (5)

9 *Annie Get Your Gun* song; '_____ Lullaby' (9)

11 Character played by Laura Dean in musical movie *Fame* (1980) (4)

13 Composer of movie *Godspell* (1973) (7,8)

14 Sky's surname in *Guys and Dolls* (9)

16 *Fiddler on the Roof* song; 'If I Were a _____ Man' (4)

19 *Blood Brothers* song; 'Easy _____' (5)

20 Lead character in *Footloose* (5)

22 Lead character in *A Greek Slave* (4)

23 *Guys and Dolls* song; 'More I Cannot _____ You' (4)

25 Director of movie musical *Tommy* (1975) (3,7)

26 *A Funny Thing Happened on the Way to the Forum* song; 'That'll _____ Him' (4)

27 *The King and I* song; '_____ Wonderful' (9)

Down

1 Lead character in *Avenue Q* (4,7)

2 Director of musical movie *Les Misérables* (2012) (3,6)

3 Actress playing Fanny Bryce in musical movie *Funny Girl* (2018) (8,5)

4 Director of movie musical *Girl Crazy* (1932); William A _____ (6)

5 Character played by Tommy Steele in musical movie *The Happiest Millionaire* (1967) (4,7)

6 *Anne of Green Gables* song; 'The _____' (5)

10 Lead character in *Mamma Mia!* played by Amanda Seyfried in 2008 movie version (6)

12 Actor playing Oliver Warbucks in musical movie *Annie* (2011) (7,6)

15 Lead character in *Guys and Dolls* played by Jean Simmons in 1955 movie version (5,5)

17 Character played by Issa Perica in musical movie *Les Misérables* (2019) (4)

18 Character played by Golshifteh Farahani in musical movie *The Music Man* (2007) (6)

21 Lead character in *Spamalot*; The Lady of the _____ (4)

22 *The Book of Mormon* song; 'Joseph Smith American _____' (5)

24 Lead character in *Fame* (4)

CROSSWORD 11

Across

1 *The 25th Annual Putnam County Spelling Bee* song; '_____ Foot' (5)

3 Director and choreographer of the musical film *Sweet Charity*, *All That Jazz* (1979) and *Cabaret* (1972) (3,5)

7 Actress playing Ali's mother in musical movie *The Music Man* (2007); _____ Taymourian (4)

9 Lead character in *Cabaret* (5,6)

10 Lead character in *Anything Goes* (4)

11 Lead character in *Fame* (7)

14 *By Jeeves* song; '_____ Boy' (5)

16 First name of lead character in *Hamilton*; _____ Hamilton (9)

17 Lead character in *Kiss Me, Kate* (4)

18 TV Show whose creators wrote *The Book of Mormon* (5,4)

20 Director of movie musical *The Fantasticks* (2000) (7,7)

22 Character played by Wilson Jermaine Heredia in musical movie *Rent* (2005) (5)

24 *Annie Get Your Gun* song; 'I Got Lost in His _____' (4)

26 First name of lead character in *A Christmas Carol* (8)

27 *Joseph and the Amazing Technicolor Dreamcoat* song; 'Close Every _____' (4)

28 *Jesus Christ Superstar* song; 'I Don't _____ How to Love Him' (4)

29 *The Sound of Music* song; 'My Favorite _____' (6)

Down

2 Writer of *Crazy for You*, George _____ (8)

4 *Name the musical movie*: A Brooklyn answering service operator becomes involved in the lives of her clients (1960) (5,3,7)

5 Lead character in *Sleeping Beauty* (5)

6 Musical with the characters Mickey, Linda, Edward, and Mrs Johnstone (5,8)

8 Lead character in *Flashdance the Musical* (4)

9 Composer of musical movie *Mary Poppins Returns* (2018); Marc _____ (7)

12 *Little Shop of Horrors* song; '_____ Row' (4)

13 Director of movie musical *Show Boat* (1936) (5,5)

15 Actor playing Benjamin Pontipee in musical movie *Seven Brides for Seven Brothers* (1954) (4,8)

19 *Oliver!* song; 'As Long as He _____ Me' (5)

21 Elle's future love in *Legally Blonde* (6)

23 Lead character in *Flashdance the Musical* (4)

25 *Titanic* song; 'No _____' (4)

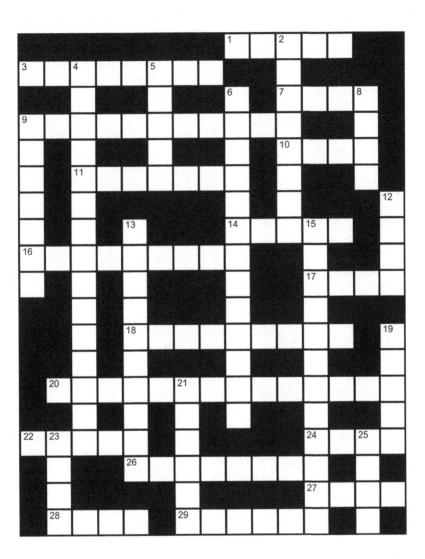

CROSSWORD 12

Across

1 Reported actor voicing Audrey II in upcoming remake of movie *Little Shop of Horrors* (5,6)

5 *Bye Bye Birdie* song; 'An English _____' (7)

6 *Grease* song; 'It's Raining on _____ Night' (4)

8 Lead character in *Dreamgirls* (5,5)

10 Director of movie musical *Cabaret* (2019); Kaustav Narayan _____ (6)

11 Character played by Alexis Smith in musical movie *Night and Day* (1946) (5,3,6)

15 *West Side Story* song; Beautiful (1,4,6)

17 Director of movie musical *Cinderella* (1977) (7,6)

18 *Seussical* song; 'Alone in the _____' (8)

21 *We Will Rock You* song; 'I Want to Break _____' (4)

22 Meg's surname in *The Phantom of the Opera* (4)

23 *A Funny Thing Happened on the Way to the Forum* song; 'That _____ Old Man' (5)

24 Lead character in *A Day in Hollywood, A Night in the Ukraine* (4)

25 Lead character in *Copacabana* (7)

26 Lead character in *The Lion King* (5)

Down

2 Butler in *The Addams Family* (5)

3 Lead character in *A Day in Hollywood, A Night in the Ukraine*; Mrs _____ (8)

4 Location of convent in *Sister Act* (3,9)

5 One of the twins in *Alice in Wonderland* (10)

7 Lead character in *Rent* (4)

9 *Chitty Chitty Bang Bang* song; 'Lovely _____ Man' (6)

12 Lead character in *Guys and Dolls*; Miss _____ (8)

13 Character played by Hermione Gingold in musical movie *The Music Man* (1962) (7,5)

14 Lead character in *13* (7)

16 *Mamma Mia!* song; '_____ You for the Music' (5)

19 *Cinderella* song; 'A Lovely _____' (5)

20 One of the characters played by David Haskell in musical movie *Godspell* (1973) (5)

21 *Name the musical movie:* A wily Roman slave schemes to earn his freedom by romantically uniting his master with a courtesan (1966); *A Funny Thing Happened on the Way to the _____* (5)

CROSSWORD 13

Across

5 *Crazy for You* song; 'Someone to _____ Over Me' (5)

8 *Name the musical movie*: A woman leaves an Austrian convent to become a governess to the children of a Naval officer widower (1965) (3,5,2,5)

9 The Genie's home in *Aladdin* (6)

10 Musical including songs 'It's the Hard Knock Life', 'Tomorrow' and 'Little Girls' (5)

11 Shakespearean play that inspired *West Side Story* (5,3,6)

14 *Name the musical movie*: As Sadie Hawkins Day approaches, Daisy Mae hopes to win the hand of a boy by catching him in the traditional race (1959) (3,5)

16 Character played by Joan Warner in musical movie *Cinderella* (1937) (7)

17 *South Pacific* song; 'This _____ Was Mine' (6)

19 Nationality of the plantation owner in *South Pacific* (6)

20 Composer of movie *West Side Story* (1961); Leonard _____ (9)

22 *South Pacific* song; 'I'm Gonna _____ That Man Right Outa My Hair' (4)

23 Director of movie musical *Oliver!* (1968) (5,4)

25 *Me and My Girl* song; 'Once You _____ your Heart' (4)

26 Character played by Philip Potter in musical movie *The Mikado* (1967) (5,3)

27 *Chitty Chitty Bang Bang* song; 'Toot _____' (6)

28 *The Rocky Horror Show* song; '_____-A Touch-A Touch Me' (5)

Down

1 Actor playing The Mikado in musical movie *The Mikado* (1939) (4,7)

2 Actor playing Riff in musical movie *West Side Story* (1961) (4,7)

3 Director of movie musical *Oklahoma!* (1955); Fred _____ (9)

4 Actor playing Motel in musical movie *Fiddler on the Roof* (1971) (7,4)

5 *The Bodyguard* song; 'I'm Every _____' (5)

6 *Waitress* song; 'It Only Takes a _____' (5)

7 Actor playing Marcellus Washburn in musical movie *The Music Man* (1962); Buddy (7)

12 Actress playing Daisy Mae Scragg in musical movie *Li'l Abner* (1959) (6,7)

13 Actor playing Christian in musical movie *Moulin Rouge!* (2001) (4,8)

15 Character played by John Savage in musical movie *Beauty and the Beast* (1987) (5)

18 Lead character in *The Fantasticks* (5)

21 Musical *Gypsy* was based on the autobiography of Gypsy _____ _____ (4,3)

22 *Into the Woods* song; 'Moments in the _____' (5)

24 Character played by Dorothy Dandridge in musical movie *Porgy and Bess* (1959) (4)

CROSSWORD 14

Across

1 Character in *Calamity Jane*; Wild Bill _____ (7)

4 Lead character in *[title of show]* (4)

7 Javert's occupation in *Les Misérables* (6)

9 Lead character in *Two Gentlemen of Verona: The Musical* (6)

11 *You're a Good Man, Charlie Brown* song; 'My New _____' (10)

12 *Peter Pan* song; 'I've Gotta ____' (4)

13 Lead character in *Waitress* (4)

15 *The Wizard of Oz* song; 'King of the ____' (6)

16 Lead character in *Moby Dick!* (7)

18 Featured character in *Cats* (7)

20 Regal title of Evelyn Oakleigh in *Anything Goes* (4)

21 Lead character in *Annie*; Daddy _____ (6,8)

23 Musical with songs 'I Could Have Danced All Night', 'The Rain in Spain' and 'Get Me to the Church on Time' (2,4,4)

25 *If/Then* song; 'You _____ to Live Without' (5)

26 Lead character in *Merrily We Roll Along*, Franklin _____ (7)

27 Actress playing Jenny Garrison in musical movie *Fame* (2009) (3,9)

Down

2 *You're a Good Man, Charlie Brown* song; 'Little _____ Facts' (5)

3 *Dirty Rotten Scoundrels* song; '_____ in a Suit' (5)

5 *Urinetown* song; '_____ your Heart' (6)

6 *Name the musical movie*: After serving time for manslaughter, young Vince Everett becomes a teenage rock star (1957) (9,4)

8 *Paint Your Wagon* song; 'I Still See _____' (5)

9 *Mary Poppins* song; 'A _____ of Sugar' (8)

10 Actor playing Lumiere in musical movie *Beauty and the Beast* (2018) (6,4)

14 Director of movie musical *Kiss Me Kate* (1953) and *Show Boat* (1951) (6,6)

17 Director of movie musical *Li'l Abner* (1959) (6,5)

18 Actress playing Belle in musical movie *Beauty and the Beast* (2017) (4,6)

19 In *Les Misérables*, Cosette 'Dreams of a castle on a _____' (5)

22 *Fosse* song; 'Big _____' (7)

23 Lead character in *An American in Paris*; ____ Davenport (4)

24 *The Full Monty* song; 'Big _____ Man' (5)

CROSSWORD 15

Across

3 *13* song; 'The _____ Place in the World' (6)

7 *Jagged Little Pill* song; 'You _____ Know' (6)

9 *Frozen* song; 'In _____' (6)

10 *Bugsy Malone* song; 'Ordinary _____' (4)

11 Starred as Dorothy in the 1978 film *The Wiz* (5,4)

14 *Sweeney Todd* song; '_____ Thing (Barber and His Wife)' (4)

15 Character played by Charles Coburn in musical movie *Gentlemen Prefer Blondes* (1953) (7,7)

18 Lead character in *Freaky Friday* (9)

19 *My Fair Lady* song; 'On the _____ Where You Live' (6)

22 Name the musical movie: Jack Skellington, king of Halloween Town attempts to bring Christmas to his home (1993); 'The _____ Before Christmas' (9)

25 George's surname in *Sunday in the Park with George* (6)

26 Green lead character in *Wicked* (7)

28 One half of the duet 'I Know Him So Well' from the original cast of *Chess* (6,5)

Down

1 *Fame* song; 'These Are My _____' (8)

2 Name the musical movie: A mysterious fair that comes to a small community in the countryside could make real the illusions of two teenagers (2000); 'The _____' (11)

4 Supporting character in *Cats*; Mr _____ (12)

5 *Bells are Ringing* song; 'Just in _____' (4)

6 Chimney sweep in *Mary Poppins* (4)

8 Character played by Howard Keel in musical movie *Annie Get Your Gun* (1950) (5,6)

12 Region led by the King in *The King and I* (4)

13 *The Wiz* song; '_____ As I Get Home' (4)

15 Lead character in *The Rocky Horror Show* played by Tim Curry in 1975 musical movie version; Dr _____-_____-_____ (5,1,6)

16 Character played by Ray Walston in musical movie *Damn Yankees* (1958); Mr _____ (9)

17 Character played by Lesley-Anne Down in musical movie *A Little Night Music* (1977) (4,7)

20 *Pinkalicious the Musical* song; 'When Dreams Come _____' (4)

21 Character played by Rita Moreno in musical movie *The King and I* (1956) (6)

23 Character played by Alan Rickman in musical movie *Sweeney Todd: The Demon Barber of Fleet Street* (2007); Judge or Lord (6)

24 Group whose music is featured in *"Mamma Mia!"* (4)

27 *Guys and Dolls* song; 'Sit Down You're Rockin' the _____' (4)

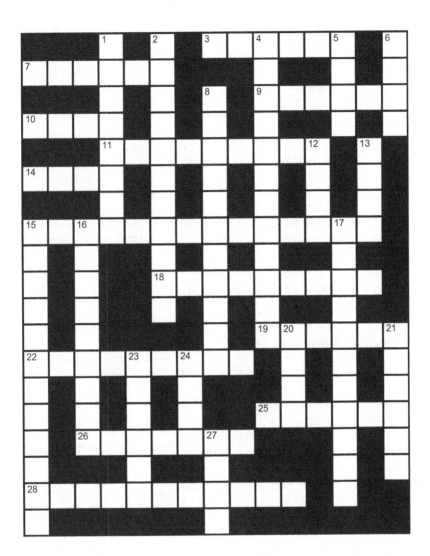

CROSSWORD 16

Across

3 Character played by John Travolta in musical movie *Grease* (1978) (5)

6 *13* song; 'All Hail the _____/Terminal Illness' (5)

8 *Lucky Stiff* song; 'The _____ Call' (5)

9 Writer of the *The Rocky Horror Show* (7,6)

12 Character played by Warner Baxter in musical movie *42nd Street* (1933) (6,5)

13 Lead character in *The Producers* (4)

14 Actor playing Cap'n Andy Hawks in musical movie *Show Boat* (1936); Charles _____ (9)

16 *Six* song; 'Don't Lose Ur _____' (4)

18 Lead character in *A Day in Hollywood, A Night in the Ukraine* (5)

20 *Man of La Mancha* song; 'The _____ Dream' (10)

24 Actor playing Claude in musical movie *Hair* (1979) (4,6)

26 *In the Heights* song; 'It Won't Be _____ Now' (4)

27 Lead character's surname in *Catch Me If You Can* (8)

Down

1 *Annie Get Your Gun* song; 'The Girl That I _____' (5)

2 Lead character in *Victor/Victoria* (5)

3 Actress playing Kathy Selden in musical movie *Singin' in the Rain* (1952) (6,8)

4 Character played by Ann Miller in musical movie *Easter Parade* (1948) (6,4)

5 *South Pacific* song; '_____ Than Springtime' (7)

6 Character played by Stellan Skarsgård in musical movie *Mamma Mia!* (2008) (4)

7 Michael's love interest in *Tootsie*; Julie _____ (7)

10 Lead character in *Oklahoma!* (3,5)

11 *South Pacific* song; 'You've Got to Be Carefully _____' (6)

12 Lead character in *The Wedding Singer* (5)

15 Lead character in *Love Never Dies* (5)

17 *Man of La Mancha* song; 'To Each His _____' (8)

18 *Titanic* song; 'To Be a _____' (7)

19 *Ghost the Musical* song; 'Unchained _____' (6)

21 *A Year with Frog and Toad* song; 'I'm Coming Out of My _____' (5)

22 Surname of character Leo in *The Producers* (5)

23 Lead character in *A Minister's Wife* (6)

25 Lead character in *Beetlejuice* (4)

CROSSWORD 17

Across

3 Lead character in *Dreamgirls* (2,5)

8 Actor playing Mikado in musical movie *The Mikado* (1967) (6,5)

11 Lead character in *Hamilton* (5)

12 Tim Rice/Andrew Lloyd Webber rock opera; *Jesus Christ* _____ (9)

13 Lead character in *Alice in Wonderland* (5)

14 Character played by Howard St John in musical movie *Li'l Abner* (1959); General _____ (9)

16 Anne's surname in *Anne of Green Gables* (7)

18 *Mary Poppins* song; 'Feed the _____' (5)

20 *Gypsy* song; 'Little ____' (4)

21 *Name the musical movie*. An ex-husband and wife team star in a musical version of *The Taming of the Shrew* (1953) (4,2,4)

24 Actor playing LeFou in musical movie *Beauty and the Beast* (2018) (4,7)

26 Lead character in *Spamalot*; Sir ____ (5)

28 Lead character in *Freaky Friday* (5)

29 *Avenue Q* song; 'I'm Not Wearing _____ Today' (9)

Down

1 Actor playing Li'l Abner Yokum in musical movie *Li'l Abner* (1959) (5,6)

2 Lead character in *Mean Girls* (4)

4 *Children of Eden* song; 'Lost in the _____' (10)

5 *Willy Wonka* song; 'Pure _____' (11)

6 Romantic lead character in *Aladdin* (7)

7 Character played by Mitzi Gaynor in musical movie *Anything Goes* (1956) (5,5)

9 *Meet Me in St Louis* song; 'The Boy _____' (4,4)

10 *The Best Little Whorehouse in Texas* song; 'The Bus from _____' (8)

15 Character played by Linda Ronstadt in musical movie *The Pirates of Penzance* (1983) (5,7)

17 Actor playing King Mongkut of Siam in musical movie *The King and I* (1956) (3,7)

19 Lead character in *Shrek the Musical* (6)

22 Character who lost his marbles in *Peter Pan* (7)

23 *Name the musical movie*: On a train trip West to become a mail-order bride, a woman meets a cheery crew of young women travelling out to open a restaurant at a remote whistle-stop (1946); *The _____ Girls* (6)

25 *Call Me Madam* song; 'Can You Use Any _____ Today' (5)

27 *Guys and Dolls* song; 'If I Were a _____' (4)

CROSSWORD 18

Across

2 Lead character in *A Don't Hug Me Christmas Carol* (6)

4 Lead character in *If/Then* (5)

7 Character played by Elton John in musical movie *Tommy* (1975); The _____ _____ (7,6)

11 *The Wizard of Oz* song; 'Ding-Dong! The _____ is Dead!' (5)

12 Dog's name in *Legally Blonde* (7)

15 *Les Misérables* song; '_____ Him Home' (5)

16 *Into the Woods* song; 'No One is _____' (5)

17 Lead character in *Starlight Express* (5)

18 Famous song from *Oliver!*; '_____, Glorious _____' (4)

19 *Honk!* song; 'Every _____ a Mother Cries' (4)

20 Lead character in *My Fair Lady* (5,7)

22 *Groundhog Day* song; 'Night Will _____' (4)

26 Lead character in *Waitress* (5)

27 *The 25th Annual Putnam County Spelling Bee* song; 'My Friend, the _____' (10)

28 *West Side Story* song; 'I Feel _____' (6)

Down

1 Director of movie musical *West Side Story* (2021); Steven _____ (9)

3 *Hedwig and the Angry Inch* song; 'Wicked Little _____' (4)

5 Actress playing Gabrielle Gerard in musical movie *The Band Wagon* (1953) (3,8)

6 Character played by Jamen Nanthakumar in musical movie *Oklahoma!* (2013) (4)

8 *Name the musical movie*: A prince cursed to spend his days as a hideous monster sets out to regain his humanity by earning a young woman's love (1991) (6,3,3,5)

9 Character played by Marion Cotillard in musical movie *Nine* (2009) (5,7)

10 Director of movie musical *A Chorus Line* (1985); Richard _____ (12)

13 Character played by Michele Lee in musical movie *How to Succeed in Business Without Really Trying* (1967) (8)

14 Nickname of character played by Charles Coburn in musical movie *Gentlemen Prefer Blondes* (1953) (5)

18 *Sweeney Todd* song; 'Green _____ and Linnet Bird' (5)

21 Musical *Hair* is based on hippies living in this city location (3,4)

23 Surname of Fanny in *Funny Girl* (5)

24 Musical including songs 'Good Morning Starshine', 'Aquarius' and 'Easy to be Hard' (4)

25 Lead character in *9 to 5* (4)

Act 2

CROSSWORD 19

Across

1 Colour of Frenchie's hair in *Grease* (4)

2 Lead character in *Love Never Dies* played by Gerard Butler in 2004 movie version (3,7)

7 *Name the musical movie*: Modern-day song-and-dance recreation of the Gospel of St Matthew (1973) (8)

9 Lead character in *The Sound of Music* (5)

10 Nationality of the nurse in *South Pacific* (8)

12 Lead character in *The Sound of Music* (5)

13 Actress playing Desiree Armfeldt in musical movie *A Little Night Music* (1977) (9,6)

18 Actress playing Cinderella in musical movie *Cinderella* (1977) (6,5)

20 *Singin' in the Rain* song; 'You Are My _____ Star' (5)

21 Lead character in *Meet Me in St Louis* (6)

22 Lead character in *Ain't Misbehavin'* (5)

25 *Hairspray* song; 'Good Morning _____' (9)

26 Character played by Kathryn Grayson in musical movie *Show Boat* (1951); Magnolia _____ (5)

27 Lead character in *1776* (4,5)

28 Character played by Marilyn Corwin in musical movie *Cinderella* (1977) (8)

Down

1 Lead character in *State Fair* (3,7)

3 Lead character in *Blood Brothers* (5)

4 *Name the musical movie*: A clever yet hapless new butler manages a Philadelphia household for quirky and joyful millionaire (1967); *The _____ Millionaire* (8)

5 Lead character in *Spring Awakening* (8)

6 *The Sound of Music* song; musical scales (2,2,2)

8 Lead character in *Spamalot*; Sir _____ (8)

11 *Name the musical movie*: Following the death of his father, an orphan is sent to live with his free-spirited aunt (1974) (4)

14 Lead character in *A Chorus Line* (4)

15 *Name the musical movie*: A rock singer travels to a small Ohio town to make his "farewell" television performance before he is drafted (1963) (3,3,6)

16 Lead character in *A Greek Slave* (10)

17 Lead character in *Ain't Misbehavin'* (7)

19 Lead character in *The Producers* (3,5)

23 *Annie Get Your Gun* song; 'My Defences Are ____' (4)

24 Rank of character played by Mitzi Gaynor in musical movie *South Pacific* (1958) (6)

26 *Amelie* song; 'Times Are ____ for Dreamers' (4)

CROSSWORD 20

Across

1 Warthog character in *The Lion King* (6)

3 Character played by Gene Kelly in musical movie *On the Town* (1949) (5)

5 *Name the musical movie*: A man leaves the family ranch in Oklahoma for New York where he is rapidly embraced into a hippie group of youngsters (1979) (4)

6 Musical that tells the story of two drag queens and a transgender woman contracted to perform a drag show at Alice Springs; _____ *Queen of the Desert* (9)

8 *Carousel* song with the lines, When You Walk Through A Storm, Hold Your Head Up High; 'You'll Never ____ Alone' (4)

9 Matron of the workhouse in *Oliver*, Mrs _____ (6)

11 Character played by Barbra Streisand in musical movie *Yentl* (1983) (5)

13 *Jekyll & Hyde* song; 'A New ____' (4)

14 *Brigadoon* song; 'I'll Go Home with ____' (6,4)

16 Actress playing Lilli Vanessi in musical movie *Kiss Me Kate* (1953) (7,7)

17 Character played by Dean Martin in musical movie *Bells Are Ringing* (1960) (7,4)

22 *Into the Woods* song; '____ in the Sky' (6)

24 Lead character in *SpongeBob SquarePants* (7)

25 *Name the musical movie*: A famous film director struggles to find harmony in his professional and personal lives (2009) (4)

26 Composer of musical movie *La La Land* (2016); Justin _____ (7)

Down

1 Location of Jean Valjean at the start of *Les Misérables* (6)

2 *Blood Brothers* song; '____ ____' (7,6)

3 *Merrily We Roll Along* song; '____ Up' (7)

4 Character played by J.K. Simmons in musical movie *La La Land* (2016) (4)

7 Musical with lyrics 'In olden days a glimpse of stocking was looked on as something shocking now heaven knows' (8,4)

9 *A Funny Thing Happened on the Way to the Forum* song; 'I'm ____' (4)

10 Character played by Richard O'Brien in musical movie *The Rocky Horror Picture Show* (1975) (4,4)

12 American musical *Oklahoma* was based on the book 'Green Grow The ____' (6)

15 Lead character in *A Christmas Story: The Musical* (4,7)

18 Country where *My Fair Lady* is set (7)

19 *Freaky Friday* song; 'No More ____' (4)

20 Lead character in *Movin' Out* (4)

21 *Pinkalicious the Musical* song; 'I Got the ____ Blues' (4)

23 *The 25th Annual Putnam County Spelling Bee* song; 'I'm Not That ____' (5)

CROSSWORD 21

Across

3 Actor playing Kenickie in musical movie *Grease* (1978) (4,7)

5 Lead character in *Bullets over Broadway* (4,5)

7 Main character in *Elf* (5)

9 Musical including songs 'Dammit, Janet!' and 'I'm Going Home'; *The _____ Horror Show* (5)

10 Beauty School Dropout in *Grease* (7)

12 Lead character in *The Boy Friend* (8,6)

14 Character played by Jane Russell in musical movie *Gentlemen Prefer Blondes* (1953) (7,4)

15 *Sunset Boulevard* song; 'Greatest _____ of All' (4)

16 Cyrano's surname in *Cyrano* (2,8)

17 Leader of the Pink Ladies in *Grease* played by Stockard Channing in 1978 movie (5)

18 Lead character in *The Wedding Singer* (6)

19 Lead character in *The Sound of Music* (5)

21 *Hedwig and the Angry Inch* song; '_____ Daddy' (5)

23 Character played by Rosemarie DeWitt in musical movie *La La Land* (2016) (5)

24 *Bye Bye Birdie* song; 'Honestly _____' (7)

25 *Bye Bye Birdie* song; 'One Last _____' (4)

Down

1 *Peter Pan* song; 'Only _____' (7)

2 Actor playing Bruno in musical movie *Fame* (1980) (3,7)

4 Lead character in *Dirty Rotten Scoundrels* (6)

6 *Fosse* song; 'Bye Bye _____' (9)

7 Actor playing Henry in musical movie *The Fantasticks* (2000) (7,6)

8 Character played by Fred Astaire in musical movie *Easter Parade* (1948) (3,5)

11 Character played by Ida Lupino in musical movie *Anything Goes* (1936) (4,8)

12 *Sweeney Todd* song; 'Worst _____ in London' (4)

13 Writer of *Oliver!* (6,4)

16 Lead character in *9 to 5* (7)

19 *Pippin* song; 'I Guess I'll _____ the Man' (4)

20 *Children of Eden* song; 'Stranger to the _____' (4)

22 *13* song; 'Being a _____' (4)

CROSSWORD 22

Across

1 Actress playing Peggy Van Alden in musical movie *Jailhouse Rock* (1957) (4,5)

6 Lead character in *Beauty and the Beast*, Prince ___ (4)

7 Candelabra in *Beauty and the Beast* (7)

8 Lead character in *The Book of Mormon* (6)

10 *Mean Girls* song; '_____ With Love' (6)

11 Lead character in *Rent* (4)

13 Head of Globalsoft's police in *We Will Rock You* (9)

16 Actress playing Tuptim in musical movie *The King and I* (2018) (2,5,4)

17 Musical that is set among the students at New York's High School for Performing Arts (4)

18 Character played by Megan Mullally in musical movie *Fame* (2009) (4,5)

23 Lead character in *Once* played by Markéta Irglová in 2007 musical movie version (4)

24 *Name the musical movie*: Armed with the titular manual, an ambitious window washer seeks to climb the corporate ladder (1967); *How to Succeed in _____ Without Really Trying* (8)

25 Song from *Once* that won the Best Original Song at the 2008 Academy Awards; 'Falling _____' (6)

26 Title of the father's fiancée in *The Sound of Music*; Elsa (8)

27 Lead character in *Fame* (4)

Down

2 Lead character in *Bullets over Broadway* (5,6)

3 *Name the musical movie*: Millie Dillmount comes to town in the roaring twenties to encounter flappers and white slavers (1967); _____ *Modern Millie* (10)

4 Lead character in *Pretty Woman: The Musical* (6)

5 *Jesus Christ Superstar* song; '_____'s Dream' (6)

6 One of the sisters in *Frozen* (4)

9 Lead character in *The Three Musketeers* (9)

11 Lead character in *The Sound of Music* (3,9)

12 Character played by Cameron Mitchell in musical movie *Carousel* (1956) (6,7)

14 Character played by Gulshan Devaiah in musical movie *Cabaret* (2019) (6)

15 Father of main character in *The Lion King* (6)

19 Lead character in *Moulin Rouge*; Harold _____ (7)

20 Lead character in *Cry-Baby the Musical* (7)

21 *Bye Bye Birdie* song; '_____, Talk to Me' (4)

22 Lead character in *A Tree Grows in Brooklyn* (5)

CROSSWORD 23

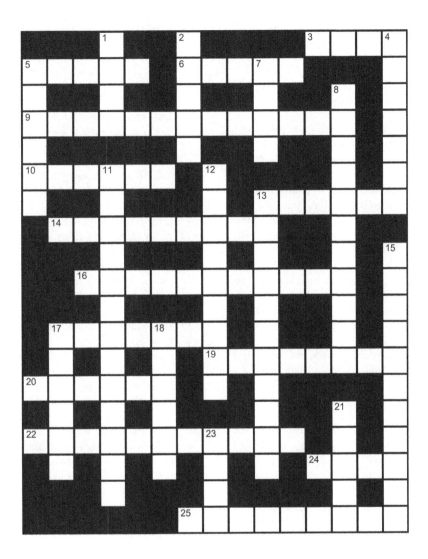

CROSSWORD 24

Across

1 *Crazy for You* song; 'Shall We ____?' (5)

4 Lead character in *Xanadu* (4)

6 Actress playing Dorothy Brock in musical movie *42nd Street* (1933) (4,7)

8 *Avenue Q* song; 'My Girlfriend, Who Lives in ____' (6)

10 Lead character in *West Side Story* (4)

11 Musical with an animal in its title won the Olivier Award for Best New Musical in 2017 (9,3)

14 *Name the musical movie*: Snobbish phonetics professor agrees to a bet that he can make a flower girl presentable in high society (1964) (2,4,4)

17 Character played by Katie Hanley in musical movie *Godspell* (1973) (5)

19 Roxie's surname in *Chicago* (4)

20 *Dreamgirls* song; 'Ain't No ____' (5)

21 *Footloose* song; 'Holding Out for a ____' (4)

22 Lead character in *Fiddler on the Roof* (7)

23 Lead character in *Meet Me in St Louis* (4)

24 Lead character in *Shrek the Musical*; Princess ____ (5)

25 Actress voicing Elsa in musical movie *Frozen* (2013) (5,6)

Down

1 Actress playing Charlotte Mittelheim in musical movie *A Little Night Music* (1977) (5,4)

2 Lead character in *Bullets over Broadway* (6)

3 Lead character in *Waitress* (5)

4 Musical with songs 'Windy City', 'Black Hills of Dakota' and 'Hive Full of Honey' (8,4)

5 Lead character (and day of the week) in *The Addams Family* (9)

7 Surname of character played by George Rose in musical movie *The Pirates of Penzance* (1983) (7)

9 Actress playing Anna Leonowens in musical movie *The King and I* (1956) (7,4)

12 Actor playing Bill Sikes in musical movie *Oliver!* (1968) (6,4)

13 Character played by Mary Tyler Moore in musical movie *Thoroughly Modern Millie* (1967) (7,5)

15 Lead character in *Meet Me in St Louis* (4)

16 Character played by Alec Baldwin in movie *Rock of Ages* (2012); Dennis ____ (6)

18 *Name the musical movie*: The Vietnam War forms the backdrop for the romance between an upper-class American girl and a poor Liverpudlian artist (2007); ____ *the Universe* (6)

21 *School of Rock* song; 'Here at ____ Green' (6)

22 *Avenue Q* song; 'A Mix ____' (4)

CROSSWORD 25

Across

1 Director of movie musical *Carousel* (1956) (5,4)

4 *The Phantom of the Opera* song; '_____ of the Night' (5)

7 Rank of character played by Wilfrid Hyde-White in musical movie *My Fair Lady* (1964) (7)

9 *Peter Pan* song; '_____ Melody' (7)

10 Actor playing Phil Davis in musical movie *White Christmas* (1954) (5,4)

12 Director of movie musical *The Producers* (2005); Susan _____ (7)

14 Lead character in *Sleeping Beauty*; The Blue ___ (4)

16 *Grease* song; 'There Are _____ Things I Could Do' (5)

17 Character played by Cyd Charisse in musical movie *Silk Stockings* (1957) (9)

19 *The Wiz* song; 'I Was _____ on the Day Before Yesterday' (4)

20 Family name of the characters in *The Sound of Music* (3,5)

22 *Kinky Boots* song; 'The History of _____ Guys' (5)

23 Character played by Richard Madden in musical movie *Rocketman* (2019) (4,4)

24 Michael's alter ego in *Tootsie* (7,8)

25 Lead character in *Bat Out of Hell: The Musical* (5)

26 *Funny Girl* song; 'Don't Rain on My _____' (6)

Down

2 *Annie* song; 'It's a Hard _____ Life' (5)

3 Lead character in *Fiddler on the Roof* played by Norma Crane in 1971 movie (5)

5 Lead character in *Moby Dick!* (7,4)

6 *The Pirates of Penzance* song; 'I Am the Very _____ of a Modern Major-General' (5)

8 Surname of character played by Carl Anderson in musical movie *Jesus Christ Superstar* (1973) (8)

11 Lead character in *The Hunchback of Notre Dame* (9)

12 Actor playing Porgy in musical movie *Porgy and Bess* (1959) (6,7)

13 Character played by Donna Murphy in musical movie *Tangled* (2010) (6,6)

14 *Honk!* song; 'You Can Play with Your ___' (4)

15 Character played by Judy Garland in musical movie *Girl Crazy* (1943) (6,4)

18 Character that puts a newt in Miss Trunchbull's glass of water in *Matilda* (8)

21 Lead character in *I Do! I Do!* (5)

CROSSWORD 26

Across

3 Musical with songs including 'Manchesterford', 'Macaroons!' and 'Tip Top Tap' (5,8)

6 *Anything Goes* song; 'Blow, _____, Blow' (7)

8 City that saw the premiere of *Les Misérables* (5)

10 Lead character in *Gentlemen Prefer Blondes* (3,6)

13 Lead character in *Jersey Boys* (7,5)

16 War that forms the basis for *Miss Saigon* (7)

19 Lead character in *Little Women* (9)

20 Lead character in *The Little Mermaid* (4)

21 Character played by Russ Tamblyn in musical movie *Seven Brides for Seven Brothers* (1954) (6)

23 Actress playing Annie in musical movie *Annie* (2011); _____ Orrell (5)

25 Lead character in *Phantom* (6)

26 Family name of main characters in *Little Women* (5)

27 *Lion King* is set in the plains of this desert (9)

Down

1 Actor playing Mr Keeney in musical movie *Funny Girl* (2018); Martin _____ (9)

2 Lead character in *Oklahoma!* played by Gordon MacRae in 1955 musical movie (5,6)

4 Musical with songs 'Maybe This Time', 'The Money Song' and 'Willkommen' (7)

5 US State where *Best Little Whorehouse* was located (5)

6 Musical including songs 'Everything's Coming Up Roses', 'Small World' and 'Together Wherever We Go' (5)

7 Character played by Gulshan Grover in musical movie *Cabaret* (2019) (3,5)

9 Main antagonist in *The Lion King* (4)

11 Lead character in *SpongeBob SquarePants* (6)

12 *The Prom* song; 'The Lady's _____' (9)

13 One of the Moe's in *Five Guys Named Moe* (4,4,3)

14 *Mary Poppins* song; '_____ can happen if you just let it' (8)

15 *Tommy* character; Cousin _____ (5)

17 Lead character in *A Christmas Story: The Musical* (3,3,3)

18 Lead character in *The Little Mermaid* (5)

22 Victor/Victoria's surname in *Victor/Victoria* (5)

24 *Guys and Dolls* song; '_____ Be a Lady' (4)

CROSSWORD 27

Across

2 *The Rocky Horror Show* song; 'Once In a _____' (5)

3 Lead character in *Hairspray* (4)

5 Lead character in *Bugsy Malone* (7)

6 Character played by Howard Keel in musical movie *Seven Brides for Seven Brothers* (1954); Adam _____ (8)

7 Lead character in *Chess*; _____ Sergievsky (7)

8 *The Little Mermaid* song; 'The _____ Above' (5)

9 Lead character in *Guys and Dolls* (3)

10 Musical with songs 'Happy Talk', 'Some Enchanted Evening' and 'I'm Gonna Wash That Man Right Outa My Hair' (5,7)

12 Mechanism of transport in *Starlight Express* (6,6)

14 Lead character in *Little Women* (3)

17 *Sunday in the Park with George* song; 'Finishing the ___' (3)

18 *Caroline, or Change* song; 'I Hate the ___' (3)

20 Millie's surname in *Thoroughly Modern Millie* (9)

22 *Urinetown* song; '___ Freedom Run' (3)

23 *Name the musical movie*: Hopefuls try out before a demanding director for a part in a new musical (1985) (1,6,4)

25 *Chicago* song; 'Funny _____' (5)

26 Story of one of America's founding fathers (8)

Down

1 Character played by Barbara Ruick in musical movie *Carousel* (1956); Carrie _____ (10)

2 *Name the musical movie*: Two youngsters from rival New York City gangs fall in love (1961) (4,4,5)

3 *Godspell* song; 'Learn Your _____ Well' (7)

4 Director of movie musical *Gentlemen Prefer Blondes* (1953) (6,5)

5 Actress playing Vera Charles in musical movie *Mame* (1974) (3,6)

11 Street where Sweeney Todd runs his barber shop (5,6)

13 *13* song; 'What it Means to Be a _____' (6)

15 Profession of the three male stars of *On the Town* (6)

16 Lead character and love interest for the soldier in *Miss Saigon* (3)

18 *Footloose* song; 'Let's Hear It for the ___' (3)

19 *The Little Mermaid* song; 'Under the ___' (3)

21 *Singin' in the Rain* song; 'Make 'Em _____' (5)

24 Lead character in *Evita* (3)

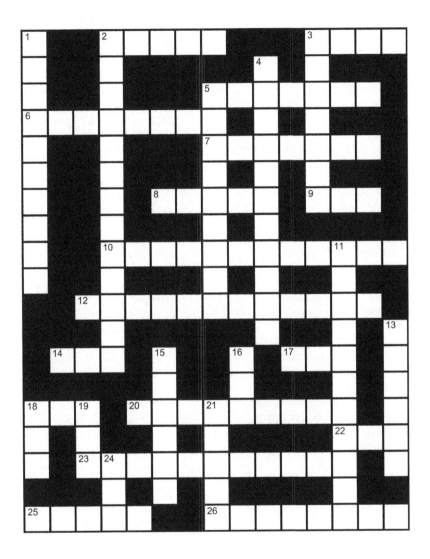

CROSSWORD 28

Across

1 *Miss Saigon* song; 'Why ___ Why?' (3)

3 *Dear Evan Hansen* song; 'So ___/ So Small' (3)

4 *Chess* song; 'I know him __ ___' (2,4)

7 *Mary Poppins Returns* song; 'The Place Where ___ Things Go' (4)

10 Musical set amidst the Bollywood film industry (6,6)

12 *Name the musical movie*: In nineteenth century London, a young girl falls for a famous womanizing criminal (1989) (4,3,5)

13 Director of movie musical *Easter Parade* (1948) and *Gigi* (1958) (7,7)

17 The youngest member of the von Trapp family; *Sound of Music* (5)

19 Four-legged animal being argued about in the opening song of *Fiddler on The Roof* (5)

20 *Blood Brothers* song; '___ Upon the Table' (5)

21 Lead character in *Fiddler on the Roof* played by Topol in 1971 movie version (5)

23 *Anything Goes* song; 'I Get a ___ Out of You' (4)

24 Sandy's surname in *Grease* (10)

27 *Kiss Me, Kate* song; 'It's Too Darn ___' (3)

28 *Always Patsy Cline* song; 'It Wasn't God Who Made Honky Tonk ___' (6)

Down

1 Actor playing Billy Bigelow in musical movie *Carousel* (1956) (6,6)

2 *Merrily We Roll Along* song; 'Not a ___ Goes By' (3)

3 Lead character in *42nd Street* (5)

5 *The Color Purple* song; 'Too Beautiful for ___' (5)

6 *The 25th Annual Putnam County Spelling Bee* song; 'I Speak Six ___' (9)

8 Character played by Roger Daltrey in musical movie *Mack the Knife* (1989) (6,6)

9 *Name the musical movie*: A frustrated fan of the hopeless Washington Senators makes a pact with the Devil to help the baseball team win the league pennant (1958) (4,7)

11 Regular musical writer partnership; Hal David and Burt ___ (9)

14 *Jane Eyre* song; 'Sweet ___' (7)

15 Musical where the words 'til we find our place, on the path unwinding' are sung (3,4,4)

16 Colour of a lead character in *Into the Woods* (3)

18 Character played by Kenneth Sandford in musical movie *The Mikado* (1967) (4-3)

22 *Fiddler on the Roof* song; 'Any Day ___' (3)

24 Lead character in *Sunday in the Park with George* (3)

25 *Kiss Me, Kate* song; 'I Hate ___' (3)

26 *The Book of Mormon* song; 'Turn it ___' (3)

CROSSWORD 29

Across

1 *Beetlejuice* song; 'Dead ___' (3)
2 Supporting character in *Avenue Q* (3)
6 *Mamma Mia!* song; 'The _____ Takes It All' (6)
8 Character played by Jamie Bell in musical movie *Rocketman* (2019); Bernie ___ (6)
10 Australian actor who won a Tony award for his role in the *Boy From Oz* (4,7)
11 Supporting character obsessed with porn in *Avenue Q* (7,7)
14 Lead character in *South Pacific* (6,7)
18 Group that had a rock opera album, associated with the musical *Tommy* (3,3)
20 *Chess* song; 'One Night in _____' (7)
21 *Annie Get Your ___* song; 'You Can't Get a Man with a Gun' (3)
22 Lead character in *BEEHIVE: The 1960's Musical* (5)
23 Lead character in *Two Gentlemen of Verona: The Musical* (7)
24 Surname of actor voicing Olaf in musical movie *Frozen* (2013) (3)
25 Actor playing Will Parker in musical movie *Oklahoma!* (1955) (4,6)

Down

1 Character played by Monty Woolley in musical movie *Night and Day* (1946) (5)
3 Family name in *Peter Pan* (7)
4 *Hair* song; 'Let the _____ in' (8)
5 Character played by Vincent Gardenia in musical movie *Little Shop of Horrors* (1986) (7)
6 Musical with lyrics 'Someday, I'll wish upon a star and wake up where the clouds are far behind me' (6,2,2)
7 Director of movie musical *Girl Crazy* (1943) (6,6)
9 Article of clothing worn by Joseph in *Jesus Christ Superstar* (4)
12 Lead character in *Footloose* (3)
13 Villain in *We Will Rock You* (6,5)
15 Character played by Taron Egerton in musical movie *Rocketman* (2019) (5,4)
16 *The Full Monty* song; 'Life With _____' (6)
17 Lead character in *Little Women* (3)
19 *The Best Little Whorehouse in Texas* song; 'Twenty-Four _____ of Lovin'' (5)
20 *Chitty Chitty Bang Bang* song; 'Doll on a Music ___' (3)
22 *Hedwig and the Angry Inch* song; '___ in a Box' (3)

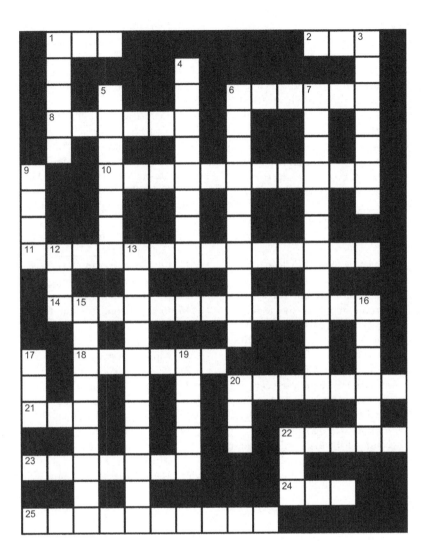

CROSSWORD 30

Across

1 Actor playing King Arthur in musical movie *Camelot* (1967) (7,6)

5 *Name the musical movie*: A successful song-and-dance team become romantically involved with a sister act; festive (1954) (5,9)

8 *Rent* song; '_____ of Love' (7)

9 *Nine* song; 'My _____ Makes Movies' (7)

10 *Honeymoon in Vegas* song; 'I Love _____' (5)

11 Lead character in *Phantom* (8)

13 Lead character in *The Boy Friend* (5,6)

15 *Urinetown* song; 'Privilege to ___' (3)

18 Character played by Angelica Serrano in musical movie *Beauty and the Beast* (2018) (6)

19 *Miss Saigon* was a rework of this Puccini work (6,9)

22 Actress playing Reno Sweeney in musical movie *Anything Goes* (1936) (5,6)

26 Lead character in *A Don't Hug Me Christmas Carol* (5)

27 Name of the man-eating plant in *Little Shop of Horrors* played by Ellen Greene in 1986 movie (6)

Down

2 Lead character in *Sweeney Todd* (7,4)

3 Director of movie musical *The Music Man* (1962); Morton _____ (7)

4 Actor playing Ali's father in musical movie *The Music Man* (2007) (6,8)

6 *Kinky Boots* song; 'Hold Me in Your _____' (5)

7 Musical with songs 'All American Prophet', 'You and Me (But Mostly Me)' and 'Baptize Me' (3,4,2,6)

10 *The Prom* song; '_____ Is Going to Prom' (5)

11 Director of movie musical *Rent* (2005); Chris _____ (8)

12 Lead character in *Moby Dick!* (3)

14 *Annie Get Your Gun* song; 'I'm a ___, Bad Man' (3)

16 *Brigadoon* song; 'Waitin' for my _____' (6)

17 Lead character in *Fame* (3)

20 King in *Spamalot* (6)

21 *Frozen* song; '___ it Go' (3)

23 Lead character in *The Producers* played by Nathan Lane in 2005 movie; _____ Bialystock (3)

24 Character played by Emma Stone in musical movie *La La Land* (2016) (3)

25 *Moulin Rouge* song; 'Come What ___' (3)

CROSSWORD 31

Across

1 US President whose reign was likened to *Camelot* (3)

3 Prince Adam's alter-ego in *Beauty and the Beast* (3,5)

7 Surname of character Billy in *Anything Goes* (7)

9 Lead character in *Sleeping Beauty*; Princess (9)

10 Family name in *Mary Poppins* (5)

12 Character played by Howard Keel in musical movie *Show Boat* (1951) (7,7)

13 *West Side Story* song; '___ Song' (3)

14 Character in *Chitty Chitty Bang Bang*; Child _____ (7)

16 *The Full Monty* song; 'Breeze Off the _____' (5)

17 *If/Then* song; 'Always _____ Over' (8)

18 Lead character in *Once* played by Glen Hansard in 2007 musical movie version (3)

19 Lead character in *Beetlejuice* (5)

22 Actor playing Jasper B Biggley in musical movie *How to Succeed in Business Without Really Trying* (1967) (4,6)

23 *Bright Star* song; 'Sun's Gonna _____' (5)

Down

1 Character played by Bert Wheeler in musical movie *Girl Crazy* (1932) (5,6)

2 Actor playing Pat Denning in musical movie *42nd Street* (1933) (6,5)

3 *Evita* song; 'On This Night of a _____ Stars' (8)

4 Country where *A Little Night Music* was set (6)

5 Musical that Benny Anderson composed music for (5)

6 Famous song from *Cats* (6)

7 Character played by Cary Grant in musical movie *Night and Day* (1946) (4,6)

8 Lead character in *Victor/Victoria* (4,7)

11 Actor playing Martin Cranston in musical movie *Fame* (2009) (6,7)

13 Lead character in *Les Misérables* played by Russell Crowe in 2012 musical movie version (6)

15 *Chess* song; 'Pity the _____' (5)

16 *Hello, Dolly!* song; '_____ Down My Back' (7)

17 Name of the flower shop's assistant in *Little Shop of Horrors* (7)

20 *The Producers* song; 'Keep It ___' (3)

21 Lead character in *Ain't Misbehavin'* (3)

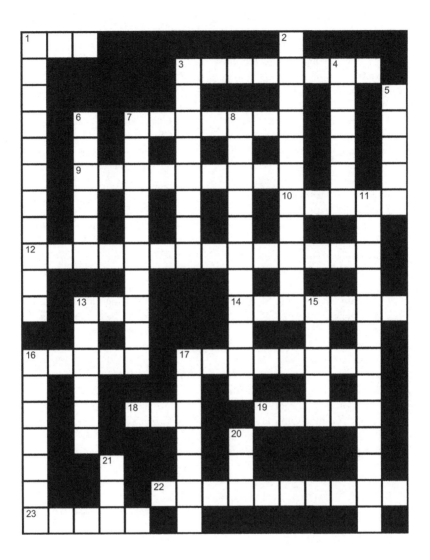

CROSSWORD 32

Across

1 Type of characters in *Avenue Q* (6)

7 *She Loves Me* song; '_____ Ice Cream' (7)

8 Lead character in *Into the Woods* (4)

9 *Sweet Charity* song; 'There's Gotta Be Something _____' (6)

10 Supporting character in *We Will Rock You* (3)

11 Character played by Ferdia Walsh-Peelo in musical movie *Sing Street* (2016) (5)

13 *The Addams Family* song; 'Just Around the _____' (6)

14 Lead character in *Hamilton* (8)

15 *The Little Mermaid* song; 'Poor _____ Souls' (11)

17 *Dear Evan Hansen* song; 'Waving Through A _____' (6)

18 Lead character in *[title of show]* (6)

20 Character played by Rachel Izen in musical movie *Funny Girl* (2018); Mrs ____ (5)

21 Musical including songs 'Not for the Life of Me', 'Forget About the Boy' and 'Gimme Gimme'; 'Thoroughly _____ Millie' (6)

23 Actor playing Florenz Ziegfeld in musical movie *Funny Girl* (2018) (5,6)

24 *Name the musical movie*: In 1850 Oregon, when a backwoodsman brings a wife home to his farm, his six brothers decide that they want to get married too (1954); _____ *Brides for* _____ *Brothers (5)*

Down

1 Actress playing Carla in musical movie *Nine* (2009) (8,4)

2 *Adding Machine: A Musical* song; 'Something to Be _____ Of' (5)

3 Lead character in *Annie Get Your Gun* (5)

4 Character played by Harve Presnell in musical movie *Paint Your Wagon* (1969); Rotten Luck _____ (6)

5 Director of movie musical *Chicago* (2002) and *Nine* (2009) (3,8)

6 Lead character in *The Rocky Horror Show* played by Susan Sarandon in 1975 movie (5,5)

9 *Spamalot* song; 'Always Look on the _____ Side of Life' (6)

12 Actor playing Larry in musical movie *A Chorus Line* (1985) (8,4)

14 Character played by Zendaya in musical movie *The Greatest Showman* (2017) (4,7)

16 *Les Misérables* song; '_____ Chairs at Empty Tables' (5)

17 Surname of lead characters in *Carrie: The Musical* (5)

19 One of Henry VIII's wives in *Six*; Katherine _____ (6)

20 *Seven Brides for Seven Brothers song;* '_____ Yore Beautiful Hide' (5)

22 Character played by Alan Jones in musical movie *Annie* (2011) (3)

CROSSWORD 33

Across

2 *Name the musical movie*: A matchmaker travels to Yonkers to find a partner for a "half-a-millionaire" (1969) (5,5)

8 Character played by Jim Broadbent in musical movie *Moulin Rouge!* (2001) (6,6)

9 *Jersey Boys* song; '_____, 1963 (Oh, What a Night)' (8)

10 Lead character in *Annie* (5)

12 Young female character in *We Will Rock You* (11)

15 *The Prom* song; 'Alyssa _____' (6)

17 *Priscilla, Queen of the Desert* song; 'I Say A Little _____' (6)

19 Lead character in *Miss Saigon* (5)

20 Actor playing The King of Siam in musical movie *The King and I* (2018) (3,8)

22 *Jersey Boys* song; 'My Eyes _____ You' (6)

23 *Bye Bye Birdie* song; '_____ Rose' (7)

24 Velma's surname in *Chicago* (5)

25 *Footloose* song; 'Can You ____ It in Your Heart' (4)

Down

1 Director of musical movie *The Greatest Showman* (2017) (7,6)

3 *Avenue Q* song; 'You Can Be as ____ as the Hell You Want' (4)

4 Director of movie musical *Godspell* (1973) (5,6)

5 *Oliver!* song; 'Consider _____' (8)

6 Lead character in *An American in Paris* (4,6)

7 James Bond actor originally cast as George in the production of *Aspects of Love*, but dropped out (5,5)

11 *Name the musical movie*: A young orphan girl's adventures in finding a family that will take her (1982) (5)

13 Composer of movie *Show Boat* (1929); Joseph _____ (11)

14 Lead character in *A Chorus Line* (6)

16 *Children of Eden* song; 'Spark of _____' (8)

17 Director of movie musical *Show Boat* (1929); Harry A _____ (7)

18 *Anne of Green Gables* song; 'The _____' (7)

19 Lead character in *Fiddler on the Roof* (5)

21 Lead character in *Movin' Out* (5)

CROSSWORD 34

Across

3 *Kismet* song; 'Stranger in _____' (8)

4 Lead character in *The Addams Family* (5)

7 One of Henry VIII's wives in *Six* (4,7)

9 First American actress to have a principal role with the Royal Shakespeare Company, in *Les Misérables* (5,6)

11 Lead character in *A Day in Hollywood, A Night in the Ukraine* (11)

12 *School of Rock* song; 'When I _____ to the Top of Mount Rock' (5)

14 Male lead character in *America's Sweetheart* (7)

15 Character played by Tommy Steele in musical movie *Finian's Rainbow* (1968) (2)

16 *Chicago* song; 'All That ____' (4)

18 Dorothy's aunt in *The Wizard of Oz* (2)

20 *Name the musical movie*: Tom the Piper's Son is about to marry Mary Quite Contrary (1961); *Babes in _____* (7)

21 *The Little Mermaid* song; 'Her _____' (5)

23 Actress playing Muzzy Van Hossmere in musical movie *Thoroughly Modern Millie* (1967); Carol _____ (8)

Down

1 Actress playing Magnolia in musical movie *Show Boat* (1936) (5,5)

2 Lead character in *Sleeping Beauty* (7)

4 Lead character in *Seussical* (8,6)

5 *Bat Out of Hell* features the songs of this artist (4,4)

6 Lead character in *The Addams Family* (8)

7 Actor playing Matt in musical movie *The Fantasticks* (2000) (4,8)

8 Last name of the minister in *A Minister's Wife* (6)

9 Actor playing Raoul in musical movie *The Phantom of the Opera* (2004) (7,6)

10 Director of movie musical *Fame* (2009); Kevin _____ (10)

13 Song from *Miss Saigon*; 'The _____ in my Mind' (5)

14 Character played by Laura La Plante in musical movie *Show Boat* (1929) (8)

17 Character that plays the electric guitar in *School of Rock* school band (4)

19 *Meet Me in St Louis* song; 'Have Yourself a _____ Little Christmas' (5)

22 Musical *Wicked* claims to be the untold story of the witches of this mythical place (2)

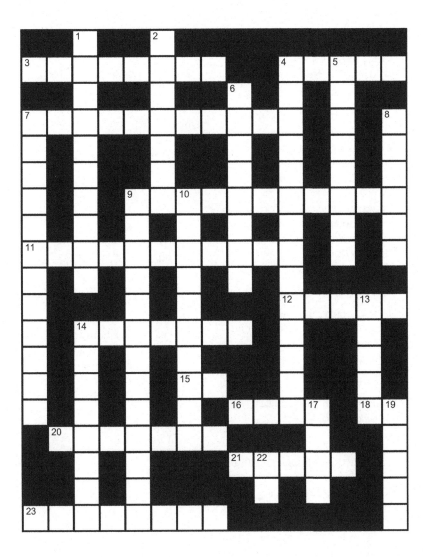

CROSSWORD 35

Across

1 *Name the musical movie*: A chronicle of the lives of several teenagers who attend a New York high school for students gifted in the performing arts (1980) (4)

3 Musical with songs 'Puttin' on the Ritz', 'I'm Putting All My Eggs in One Basket' and 'Let's Face the Music and Dance' (3,3)

7 Lead character in *Starlight Express* (5)

8 *Name the musical movie*: A female girlie club entertainer in Weimar Republic era Berlin romances two men (1972) (7)

9 Actress playing Rosie DeLeon in musical movie *Bye Bye Birdie* (1963) (5,5)

12 Lead character in *Dreamgirls* (7)

13 Activity that Tracy takes part in on The Corny Collins Show (*Hairspray*) (7)

14 Director of movie musical *Fame* (1980) (4,6)

15 Director of movie musical *The Mikado* (1939); Victor _____ (12)

19 Lead character in *West Side Story* played by Rachel Zegler in 2021 movie (5)

20 *Ragtime* song; 'Night that _____ Spoke in Union Square' (7)

22 Character played by Robert E Strickland in musical movie *Girl Crazy* (1943) (5,7)

23 Director of movie musical *Cinderella* (2016); Chance _____ (6)

24 TV show that actress playing Ms Kraft in musical movie *Fame* (2009) starred in (6)

Down

2 Actress playing Velma Von Tussle in musical movie *Hairspray* (2007) (8,8)

4 Director of movie musical *Cinderella* (1937) (6,5)

5 Annual awards for distinguished achievement in American theatre (4)

6 Elle's ex-boyfriend in *Legally Blonde* (6)

9 Lead character in *42nd Street* (6)

10 *Hello Dolly* is based on this play (3,10)

11 Lead character in *Les Misérables* played by Anne Hathaway in 2012 musical movie version (7)

13 Lead character in *The Wiz* (7,4)

16 *A Little Night Music* song; 'The _____ Life' (9)

17 Ghost lead character in *Ghost the Musical* (3,5)

18 Character played by Michael Blevins in musical movie *A Chorus Line* (1985) (4)

21 *Cinderella* song; 'In My Own _____ Corner' (6)

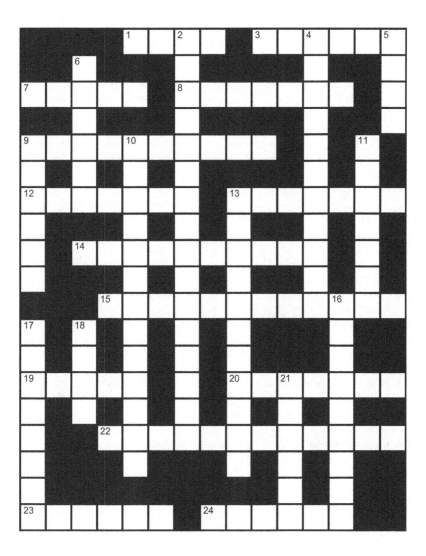

CROSSWORD 36

Across

5 Director of movie musical *Cinderella* (2016) and *Oklahoma!* (2013) (6,5)

6 Character played by Stanley Holloway in musical movie *My Fair Lady* (1964) (6)

7 First name of lead character in *Chaplin: The Musical* (7)

9 Actor playing Gaston in musical movie *Beauty and the Beast* (2017) (4,5)

12 *Ghost the Musical* song; 'I Can't _____' (7)

14 Character played by James Mason in musical movie *A Star Is Born* (1954) (6,5)

15 Actor playing Lancelot Du Lac in musical movie *Camelot* (1967) (6,4)

17 *42nd Street* song; '_____ Of Broadway' (7)

19 *Annie Get Your Gun* song; 'They Say It's _____' (9)

20 Lead character in *Fiddler on the Roof* (5)

21 Lead character in *Two Gentlemen of Verona: The Musical* (5)

22 *A Christmas Carol* song; '____ By ____' (4)

23 Character played by Yana Nirvana in musical movie *Cinderella* (1977) (8)

Down

1 Character played by Michael York in musical movie *Cabaret* (1972); ____ Roberts (5)

2 Character played by Anthony 'Scooter' Teague in musical movie *How to Succeed in Business Without Really Trying* (1967) (3,5)

3 Director of movie musical *Bells Are Ringing* (1960), *Gigi* (1958) and *The Band Wagon* (1953) (8,8)

4 Actress playing Ruth in musical movie *The Pirates of Penzance* (1983) (6,8)

8 Lead character in *Dirty Rotten Scoundrels* (8)

10 Actress playing Machekha in musical movie *Cinderella* (1961) (5,5)

11 *Company* song; 'The Ladies Who _____' (5)

13 Character played by Takao Osawa in musical movie *The King and I* (2018) (3,9)

15 Lead character in *9 to 5* (8)

16 Lead character in *Cabaret* (8)

18 Lead character in *Movin' Out* (6)

Encore

CROSSWORD 37

Across

1 *The Wiz* song; 'The _____ We Once Had' (7)
8 Lead character in *Sweeney Todd* (7)
9 Lead character in *Spring Awakening* (6)
11 Composer of musical movie *Moulin Rouge!* (2001); Craig _____ (9)
12 Character played by Charlie Barnick in musical movie *Cinderella* (2016) (6)
13 Actress playing Kate in musical movie *Oklahoma!* (2013) (8,5)
16 Actor playing Maximilian von Heune in musical movie *Cabaret* (1972) (6,5)
18 Male character in *Frozen* (8)
20 Lead character in *Beauty and the Beast* played by Rebecca Jimenez in 2018 movie (5)
21 Composer of musical movie *Frozen* (2013); _____ Anderson-Lopez (7)
22 *Sweet Charity* song; '_____ of Life' (6)
23 *My Fair Lady* song; 'I'm an _____ Man' (8)

Down

2 *Rent* song; 'One Song _____' (5)
3 Lead character in *Funny Girl* (5,5)
4 Writer of musical movie *Aladdin* (2019) (4,6)
5 Director of movie musical *The Music Man* (2007) (7,7)
6 Lead character in *Into the Woods* (3,5)
7 Lead character in *Willy Wonka JR* (7,3)
10 Lead character in *Hamilton* (5,4)
14 Matron in *Chicago* (4,6)
15 Musical including the song *Pinball Wizard* (5)
16 Lead character in *An American in Paris*; Adam _____ (8)
17 Character played by Jane Powell in musical movie *Seven Brides for Seven Brothers* (1954) (5)
19 *Jane Eyre* song; 'The _____ Things' (5)

Solutions

Crossword 1

```
    T R O L L E Y     H O M E
  Z   O A   E         A   L
  U   U K   V         N   L
  K   L I L L I   J   N   E
J O J O   E   S H E R I D A N
O     U Y   T   A G   N
S     S   U   N   A N N E
E     E M A B E L   N   M
P H I L I A   B   O       I
H     A   R E S C U E     L
C     U T     I     L I L Y
A     T Y     S       E
B A H R A M R A D A N     R
L     E   A L
E R I C I D O L   B L O N D E
  I   I     E       E
    S U S A N       L
    O   O   D O L L S
L I G H T N I N G
```

Crossword 2

```
T O M M Y A L B R I G H T   T
R   A                       Y
E   C Y N D I L A U P E R
E   H   E       N   A   O
S   E Y E S     T   T   N
    A   M A D H A T T E R
  T H E E N G I N E E R   S
  H   L   D   Y   E   A
T I M M Y   G A R Y C L A R K
  N   E       A   A   I
  E   R O C K   P O R T H O S
W B   E     P   I   D
I E   B   N     O L A F
C A T H E R I N E   N   W
K H   A   C   N   S   S
E   H U N K H O U G H T O N
D   T   I   C   I   N
  B O Y L E   H A P P Y
```

Crossword 3

```
  C I R C L E             N   R
A   O   I   G R A N D M A     O
R E G I N A         E   G   B
O   E   D   D   L A U R A   E
U   R   A   I       T   S   R
S   E       R O X I E H A R T
E     W     T       R K   D
L I B R A R Y   E P O N I N E
  A   L   D   U   N       L
J O N A T H A N G R O F F   A
O   N   E   N   E   M   I   M
S   I   R   C A N D Y   N   E
H   S   M   I   E       I   R
  P T B A R N U M   L E A V E
    E   T   G   A   E   N
S T R A T     R O S E   J
O       H E L E N   T   A
N       A   E V E N I N G
G   T H U N D E R   R   E
```

Crossword 4

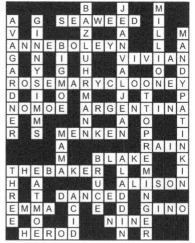

```
              B     J     M
A   G S E A W E E D   I
V   I     Z   A       L   M
A N N E B O L E Y N   L   A
G   N I   U   V I V I A N D
A   Y G   H   A     O   D
R O S E M A R Y C L O O N E Y
D   I O   M   J   T   P
N O M O E   A R G E N T I N A
E   M N     A   O   T
R   S   M E N K E N   P   I
        A       R A I N
        M   B L A K E   K
T H E B A K E R   L   M
H   A       U   A L I S O N
R   T D A N C E D   N
E M M A   C   D   G I N O
E   O   I   N I N E
  H E R O D       N   R
```

Crossword 5

Crossword 6

Crossword 7

Crossword 8

Crossword 9

Crossword 10

Crossword 11

Crossword 12

Crossword 13

J R Z L W A T C H
O U I E O A A
T H E S O U N D O F M U S I C
N S N N A T K
B O T T L E A N N I E E
A A M R T
R O M E O A N D J U L I E T
C B N F E W
L I L A B N E R S A
A Y E E V E L Y N E
Y N E A R L Y I M
S U F R E N C H
B E R N S T E I N P G
O S A R
W A S H C A R O L R E E D
O E B R G
O L O S E N A N K I P O O
D E S S R
S W E E T S T O U C H

Crossword 14

H I C K O C K J E F F J
N H O A
P O L I C E S I L V I A
M W M L P L L
A N P H I L O S O P H Y
R S O W O
C R O W D A W N U
O G F O R E S T
I S H M A E L U E
C E O E L E C T R A
A L O R D M L O
N V G M O C
O L I V E R W A R B U C K S
N S W D P
M Y F A I R L A D Y B E
I R D T L N
L E A R N S H E P A R D
O N E O C E
K A Y P A N A B A K E R

Crossword 15

C F L A M E S T B
O U G H T A I I E
I N F S U M M E R
F O O L T R T E T
D I A N A R O S S S
P O O R S N F I O
E T K F A O
F R A N C I S B E E K M A N
R P C U L N
A P K A T H E R I N E
N L S L E E
K E E S T R E E T
N I G H T M A R E R G U
F A U B U E P
U T R B S E U R A T
R E L P H A B A M I
T I O A M
E L A I N E P A I G E N
R T

Crossword 16

M T D A N N Y
B R A I N P H O N E A O
I R I D B D U
L R I C H A R D O B R I E N
L Y H D Y I N G
O O E E E
T J U L I A N M A R S H R
A U S N E A
U L L A N Y L
G I W I N N I N G E R
H E A D E O A
T U C A R L O O
M L A D U
E C I M P O S S I B L E
L I T H L U
J O H N S A V A G E L O N G
D E D I L O E
Y A B A G N A L E M N
M E

Crossword 17

Crossword 18

Crossword 19

Crossword 20

Crossword 21

Crossword 22

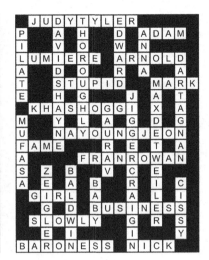

Crossword 23

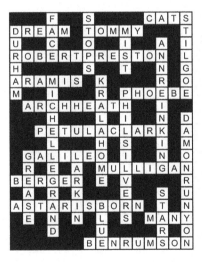

Crossword 24

Crossword 25

```
H E N R Y K I N G   M U S I C
      N     O             I         C
M   C O L O N E L     I           P
O         C       D I S T A N T
D A N N Y K A Y E   C       A     I
E                   A             N
L   Q       S T R O M A N         A
  F A U N   G   I   I   O   A
    O   A   I   D   O   T   H
W O R S E   N I N O T C H K A
    D   I   G   E       E     B
L   M   E   Y   B O R N
A   V O N T R A P P       G   A
V   D   G   O     W R O N G   N
E   J O H N R E I D       T   N
N         A   T         H   E
D O R O T H Y M I C H A E L S
E             E       L
R A V E N   P A R A D E
```

Crossword 26

```
            C           C
A C O R N A N T I Q U E S       S
  A         L     E     R
G A B R I E L   X     L     D
Y   A       A   A     Y     O
P A R I S   G U S E S M O N D
S   E   C   H   U   C     S   A
Y   T   A   A   G   L     A
    I   F R A N K I E V A L L I
    M   O   N   E       I   I
    P U Y   V I E T N A M   R
    R   R   T   I   H     R
J O S E P H I N E   E R I C
V   Y   I       O   E
G I D E O N   G   L I L L Y
N     D   G E R A R D     U
G     M       A   N   A   H
      O       N       A   K
S E R E N G E T I     N
```

Crossword 27

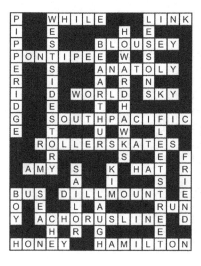

```
P       W H I L E       L I N K
I       E       H   E
P       S   B L O U S E Y
P O N T I P E E   W   S
E       S       A N A T O L Y
R       I       A   R   N
I       D   W O R L D   S K Y
D       E       T   H
G       S O U T H P A C I F I C
E       T   U   W   L
        R O L L E R S K A T E S
        R       S   E     F
A M Y   S   K   H A T     R
        A   I   S     I
B U S   D I L L M O U N T   E
O   E   L   A       R U N   D
Y   A C H O R U S L I N E
    H   R   G       E
H O N E Y       H A M I L T O N
```

Crossword 28

```
  G O D   B I G   S O W E L L   L
  O   A   I       O     O       A
  R   Y   L O S T   R   D       N
  D       L   T   D   D         G
B O M B A Y D R E A M S         U
  N   A       E   M             A
  M A C K T H E K N I F E       G
  A   H       T   Y     E       E
  C H A R L E S W A L T E R S
  R   R   I   N   H   E
  A   A   B   N   K   E   D
  E   C   E   G R E T L   I
P     H O R S E   E
O       T   R   S H O E S
O   T E V Y E   N     N
H           O       K I C K
B   D U M B R O W S K I   N
A   O   E   F       N
H O T   N   F   A N G E L S
```

Crossword 29

Crossword 30

Crossword 31

Crossword 32

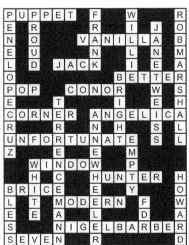

Crossword 33

```
      M H E L L O D O L L Y
L   I       O   A       O
I   C   R   U   V       U
S   H A R O L D Z I D L E R
E   A   G       D       R S
D E C E M B E R   G R A C E
A   L   R       R   R   N F
S   G   M       E   E   N
S C A R A M O U C H E   I
I   A   O   H   N   E   N C
N   C   G R E E N E       A
    E   E   R       C     S
P R A Y E R     N   C H R I S
O   P       I   H   E     I
L   O   K E N W A T A N A B E
L   L   D     V   V   T
A D O R E D     S P A N I S H
R   G   I       K     O
D   Y   K E L L Y   F I N D
```

Crossword 34

```
    I   M
P A R A D I S E       G O M E Z
    E   N     M     E   E
J A N E S E Y M O U R   A   M
O   E   R       R   T   T   O
E   D   T       T   R   L   R
Y   U   P A T T I L U P O N E
M   N   A   A   C   D   A   L
C O N S T A N T I N E   F   L
I   E   R   C   A   M
N   I   H         C L I M B
T   M I C H A E L   F   O
Y   A   K   R       U   V
E   N   I   E   O G   Z   I
E   N   I   E   J A Z Z   E M
  T O Y L A N D       A     E
  L   S       V O I C E     R
  I   O       Z   K       R
C H A N N I N G             Y
```

Crossword 35

Crossword 36

Crossword 37

FEELING   F   J
        L D A   O
T G   JOHANNA H
H R   R R N   N
E A   Y I Y   A
WENDLA U B   U
I D ARMSTRONG
TOPHER H I   U
C A O   M C   S
H JENNIFEREMETT
  O B   H A   O
 HELMUTGRIEM   M
 O R   J A   M
 C M R U M   Y
 H I KRISTOFF
 BELLE   R I
 E L KRISTEN
 RHYTHM   O E
 G   ORDINARY

ABOUT THE AUTHOR

Kyle loves puzzles and sharing them with others. Check out the Kyle Becker author page on Amazon for more in this series. New puzzle books are added regularly.

Happy Puzzling!